RAILWAY W

by
MARTIN GREEN

Cam Station Pub
Dursley Branch

Twelve Circular Walks along abandoned Railway lines in Gloucestershire, Wiltshire and Oxfordshire

Published
by
REARDON PUBLISHING
PO Box 919
Cheltenham, GL50 9AN
England
www.reardon.co.uk
Email: reardon@bigfoot.com

Written and Researched
by
Major Martin Green
2nd Edition 2009
Copyright © 2003

ISBN 1 873877 61 7
ISBN(13) 978 1873877 61 6
Design and Layout
by
Nicholas Reardon

Cover Design
by
Peter T Reardon

Photographs
by
John Plant and Roger Ashdown

Line Drawings
by
Peter T Reardon

Printed in Cheltenham

RAILWAY WALKS

Twelve Circular Walks along abandoned Railway lines in
Gloucestershire, Wiltshire and Oxfordshire

by
MARTIN GREEN

CONTENTS

INTRODUCTION

England used to enjoy one of the most comprehensive railway networks in Europe. By the last decade of the Nineteenth Century there was hardly a hamlet in the land which could not be reached by train itself or after a brief ride in a pony and trap from the nearest station. However, the improved reliability and sheer convenience of internal combustion engined road vehicles brought competition to the railways which caused a steady and persistent decline in freight and passengers throughout the second half of the Twentieth Century. By then the railways, initially funded by private enterprise, had been nationalised as a state asset. This left the state paying for trains which ran at a loss for lack of goods and people to fill them. During the late 1950's and throughout the 1960's successive governments sought to staunch this outflow of funds by closing thousands of miles of railway lines and hundreds of stations. Many of these were branch lines, that is a track leaving the main line to serve a specific place but going no further. At a stroke large parts of the huge Nineteenth Century civil engineering effort which went into building the network were redundant and, once any salvage of value was removed, duly abandoned. By and large it was not economic to reinstate the cuttings, embankments and bridges built to give the most straight and level route possible for each line.

What is left of these abandoned lines can offer rewarding walks through the heart of the countryside, away from roads and traffic, rich in flora and fauna and littered with dramatic examples of Victorian civil engineering. In short there is something to the taste of the routine walker and the railway enthusiast. For either type they are best done twice, once in summer and once in winter. The summer will show what grows where the plough and the sprayer do not go. The winter will show the detail of what was built, well over a century ago.

It does now seem certain that the wonderful convenience of the motor car and the lorry is taking a toll on the environment which can not be paid indefinitely. The sight of narrow lanes during the rush to work jammed with four and a half litre engined cars carrying just the driver is common in Gloucestershire. The four and a half litres might be better employed in a railbus taking 20 people to work along the forgotten branch line just behind the hedge.

MIDLAND & SOUTH WESTERN JUNCTION RAILWAY (MSWJR)

BACKGROUND INFORMATION

The MSWJR ran from Cheltenham to Andover through Gloucestershire, Wiltshire and Hampshire with principal intermediate stations at Cirencester, Swindon and Marlborough. Connections were available at either end to as far afield as Edinburgh and Paris. MSWJR was a precise name because the line joined the Midland Railway at the north end with the London and South Western Railway to the south. This north/south junction was an important element of the business hopes which motivated the founders of the line. It offered a direct route from the industrial south west Midlands to the port of Southampton to rival the line through Oxford, Newbury and Winchester. The project was completed in fits and starts due to a combination of under capitalisation, incompetent contractors and obstructive tactics from the Great Western Railway (GWR) who had an existing line between Swindon and Gloucester from which the MSWJR might have taken business. The section Swindon to Marlborough was opened in 1881. In 1883 the lines from Marlborough to Andover and Swindon to Cirencester came into use. In 1891 the final section which demanded the most challenging civil engineering through the Cotswold Hills between Cirencester and Cheltenham was completed and the route operated as a single business entity.

It was not hugely profitable and never repaid the capital risked by the share holders but did offer some useful passenger services. Cheltenham to Andover was routinely run in less than an hour and three quarters, Cheltenham to Southampton in two and a half hours. Those times would not be achieved by road in the rush hour today. Freight traffic amounted to 50% of the MSWJR annual revenue in most years but did not develop as well as had been anticipated. By chance rather than business acumen the most profitable periods for the line came in wartime - the Boer War, the Great War and the Second War. Then the track really hummed as men and materials from all points north flooded into Southampton for transport overseas. In the Great War it is recorded that over three million men and one hundred and thirty thousand horses were carried between Cheltenham and Andover as well an inestimable tonnage of war stores. In 1923, under the regrouping provisions of the 1921 Railways Act, the MSWJR was disbanded and the assets vested in the GWR, the old business rival. Closure of the route was similar to the construction, done bit by bit but effectively complete by 1966. With a certain irony, however, the 5 mile section running west from Andover to the Ministry of Defence supply depot and Royal Engineers railway training camp at Ludgershall is maintained intact for military use only.

WITHINGTON
(near Cheltenham, Gloucestershire)

Ordnance Survey Map Sheet Outdoor Leisure 45
Distance 4 miles

Take the A436 road signed to Gloucester where it joins the A40 Oxford to Cheltenham road 1 mile south east of Andoversford. After 3/4 of a mile turn left at the cross roads onto the minor road signed for Withington.

After precisely 2 straight miles the first premises in Withington on this north western approach, the boldly signed Manor Farm, are on the right. Almost at once a stone track appears on the left. It was the entrance road to Withington station situated between Andoversford and Chedworth stations on the MSWJR. At the right side of the road/track junction is a broad grass verge on which to park. The station opened in 1891 and closed in 1961, for the final 5 years it was only a halt. At the time it was most used over 2000 tickets were sold and 1300 tons of freight shifted annually.

The Down Platform, Withington Station

Take the stone track towards two immediately visible metal gates. The left was the station entrance, now closed to the public. The foot path goes through the right hand gate to an occupation overbridge. The upper surfaces of the all brick bridge are in fair condition but the inner arch is deteriorating. Over the left parapet the track bed and platforms are visible under ivy and a vigorous copse of young ash. Over the right parapet the track bed for the double line and the sides of the station cutting are obvious. The bridge descends into a plantation of mixed deciduous trees through which the path is well marked by yellow Cotswold Warden arrows. Go through the hunt gate from the plantation into the permanent pasture and cross the field directly then turn sharp right after the stile. To the front is an occupation underbridge constructed with a mixture of brick and local stone. Enter the kissing gate and go under the bridge through the substantial railway embankment. The path now becomes a trench spanned by two foot bridges and revetted with Cotswold stone passing through the rectory garden of the church of St Michael and All Angels. Both church and rectory are on the right. The path was sunk in the Eighteenth Century to provide privacy from walkers for the rectory ground floor rooms and the garden. The much later arrival of railway carriages slowing along the tall embankment into the station roundly defeated this aim.

Turn left where the path joins the village street and follow the road downhill past the Mill Inn. At the far left hand corner of the inn car park a brick culvert gives passage under the embankment to the infant River Colne. Very close inspection of the culvert is easy. It is in exceptional condition and of fine workmanship. Continue to follow the road past the one surviving brick abutment of an underbridge on the right and enter the car park of the Jubilee Village Hall, also on the right, as the ground rises The hall was built on the track bed of the disused line in 1977. Follow the concrete slab path beside the wall of the hall nearest the road. It leads into a deep cutting. The Cotswold stone sides show what hard labour it would have been to dig with nothing but pick axes and crowbars. Stay on the line until it is crossed by a plain wire fence then turn left over the wooden stile onto the lane and turn right down hill. The lane passes between the tall brick and local stone abutments of an underbridge. They have been repaired and re-capped since the span itself was removed, before this they were even higher. Once through the bridge there is a local stone embankment retaining wall on the left.

Continue along the lane then turn left on the stone track beneath the intact occupation underbridge. It is in fine order and the brick/local stone design of the abutment faces is almost decorative. The track veers right after the bridge. Follow the footpath sign left over the wood and railway sleeper stile. The latter are survivors from the dismantling of the line. The path is now liberally signed over permanent pasture via two further stiles, one with more sleepers, through a hazel and thorn coppice then via a kissing gate onto a steep bank. Follow the wire fence on the left then take the wooden stile over the field wall.

Occupation Bridge, Withington

The railway continued to Chedworth along the contour just inside the tree line on the opposite side of the valley to the right. It is visible after leaf fall. The path, now a generous grass strip, follows the headland, turns right at the corner of the field through a five bar gate thence over a stile to the River Colne. Take the foot bridge over the river, turn left after the stile and follow the river bank then turn left again after the stile onto the lane. Stay on the lane as it rises gently to the crest overlooking Withington then descends steeply to the King's Head Inn. Turn left at the T junction and continue through the village. The Jubilee Village Hall appears on the left and the route out may be used to return to the starting point. Alternately go straight past the entrance to the sunken rectory path leaving St Michael's on the right and the parking place appears almost at once. Behind it is a fine view of the Cotswolds to the north west showing what a scenic ride the MSWJR offered on this section. The sheer engineering effort on the mile of line into and out of Withington is remarkable. It runs in a cutting or on an embankment nearly all the way and required a major culvert, an overbridge and four underbridges. Most of this is still there to see and explore.

SOUTH CERNEY
(near Cirencester, Gloucestershire)

Ordnance Survey Map Sheet Explorer 169
Distance 5 miles

Take the B4696 'Spine Road' signed to Ashton Keynes from the junction with the A419 road some 3 and a half miles south of Cirencester. Take the first right 'Station Road' signed to South Cerney. Entering the speed limit for the village the road curves left and just before the houses begin there is a broad tarmac entrance to a disused gravel pit on the left in which to park. Immediately opposite on the right hand side of the road is a red brick 10 arched bridge to carry Wildmoorway Lane over the MSWJR line. Beside the lane is a green signed public bridle way which leads under the bridge. Take the lane to the high point of the bridge. Visible on the left is a new housing estate which covers the site of South Cerney station, intermediate between Cricklade and Cirencester Watermoor stations. To the right, indeed all around,are gravel pits, some active others disused and filled with water. The station opened in 1883 when the line reached no further north than Cirencester. Freight was the main function with milk from the surrounding dairy farms and gravel providing reliable if undramatic income for the station right up to closure in 1963.

Return to Station Road and take the public bridleway. It leads under the bridge which is a fine piece of Victorian workmanship with decorative oblong cut outs in the arch uprights. The bricks at the ends of the cut outs are slightly raised under the arches through which the line itself passed. It seems now an almost grandiose bridge for Wildmoorway Lane which degenerates into a foot path within a quarter mile. When it was built Station Road came to the end of the bridge most distant from the parking place so the bridge carried the southern access to the village. Station Road was realigned to make way for the gravel pit now signed as 'Andrew's Lake' after the MSWJR was abandoned. The bridle path emerges from the bridge onto what was a platform and descends down the platform ramp onto the line. The unmistakable tapered concrete railway boundary posts posts remain in the hedge on the right. Leaving the housing estate and a play ground, once the large goods yard, on your left continue over the rather worn red brick culvert carrying the River Churn. Two more minor culverts follow then another 10 arch bridge carrying Bow Wow lane over the line. It is almost identical to the station bridge differing only in a little local stone being used in the arch faces. Bow Wow lane also becomes merely a foot path. It may be that the generous design of these bridges was demanded by the soft, low lying land on which they are built. Two simple earth ramps leading to a single arch might have been vulnerable to subsidence while the large foot print of the 10 arches would exert less ground pressure. The line now becomes an embankment from which All Hallows church tower is visible on the left. After one more culvert take the path cut into the embankment on the left and cross the wooden stile then turn right through the brick and local stone foot path underbridge. The embankment continues towards Cirencester. Enter the permanent pasture over the stile immediately after the bridge and make straight for the far left hand corner of the field passing under the power lines. Cross the stone stile in the hedge and turn right on the tow path of the canal which ran from Upper Framilode on the Severn to Lechlade on the Thames linking these two navigable rivers. There is a daunting project to reopen this canal. Follow the canal as it meanders along a contour to Bow Wow lane. From late January to mid February the wood on the right of the tow path as it nears the lane offers a spectacular display of wild aconites. Cross the lane and follow the unusual cut and laid willow hedge to Boxwell Spring Lock where there is a useful canal information board. Continue along the tow path through the stile beside the metal gate and pass the much deeper and very dilapidated Humpback Lock. Shortly after it the remains of the red brick bridge which carried Wildmoorway Lane over the canal are visible on the right. The next lock is Wildmoorway Lower which boasts a bridge fully restored in 1996. Cross the Spine Road by the stiles provided and follow the finger posts to Cerney Wick along the tow path. When the canal and the railway were in use there was no Spine Road, merely a foot path here,hence the canal bridge. Turn right onto the lane at the next lock, Cerney Wick, leaving the lock keepers cottage on the left.

Turn left at the 'T' junction beside the Crown Inn and stay on the lane as it serpentines through the outskirts of Cerney Wick. When well clear of the village the lane ascends a MSWJR overbridge. Turn left down the stone track on the far side of the bridge and left again after 200 yards through the gap in the hedge over the gravel hump. Turn left on the railway line itself. The bridge is very similar to those already encountered but has only 9 arches. The bricks are deteriorating but repairs have been made to the points of some arches. Follow the line through the bridge and soon after the remains of a farm occupation level crossing metal gate are on the right. It was one of four hung in pairs used to prevent livestock from wandering up or down the line when they were driven across it from field to field. The track continues for a straight mile passing another farm level crossing then reaches the Spine Road. Here is yet another fine 10 arch brick overbridge sitting redundant by the roadside. When built it carried a one track lane which ended in a 'T' junction the cross of which was Station Road left and Cerney Wick right. The bridge is well exposed for examination and the raised bricks decorating top and bottom of the cut outs are obvious. The remains of insulated telegraph wire carriers are visible on the wall of one arch. The arches are not all aligned which has an odd visual effect. Go under the bridge and through the wicket gate back onto the line where the waters of disused gravel pits lap at the track bed on both sides.

When Station Road is reached in half a mile turn left on the gravel path inside the post and rail fence. It leads straight back to the parking place.

Bow Wow Lane Bridge, South Cerney

THE CIRENCESTER BRANCH LINE
(near Cirencester, Gloucestershire)

Ordnance Survey Map Sheet Explorer 169
Distance 3 and a half miles

Take the A429 road towards Kemble from the junction with the A433 road,1 and a half miles south west of Cirencester. Take the first left signed to Ewen. After a 1/4 mile the lane dips beneath a three arch underbridge of local stone at Ewen Wharf. The lane rises away from the bridge and there is a casual lay by on the left with room to park one vehicle. Walk back towards the bridge and before reaching it scramble up the track beside the abutment on the left hand side. Once on the embankment turn right to continue along the Cirencester Branch. Opened in May 1841 it is the oldest line dealt with in this book. Controlled by the Great Western Railway (GWR) it ran from Cirencester, where the imposing Town Station still stands,to Kemble where it joined the Gloucester/Swindon main line. By 1865 Cirencester to London Paddington took 2 hours 20 minutes and by 1923 that was down to 2 hours 5 minutes. Point to point that time would be hard to better by road or rail today. The line was closed in 1965 after a brief trial with an early type of diesel railbus. At the height of the branch's popularity the annual business at Cirencester included over 48,000 tickets sold, 165,000 gallons of milk and 16,000 smaller items of freight transported with over 2,200 wagons full of livestock from the nearby market.

The underbridge had three arches to allow for the lane, a pavement and the Severn Thames canal which is visible over left and right parapets, hence Ewen Wharf. On the right is a brick canal occupation bridge which was rebuilt in 1997. The GWR bought out the canal company although it offered only feeble competition to the branch for freight work. There is a frequently stated plan to reopen the complete Severn Thames canal link. Between the original wire fences with a mix of railway tapered concrete and recycled sleeper uprights the line enters a shallow cutting past the brick foundation of a line maintenance hut on the right. At the deepest point the cutting is spanned by an overbridge of mixed local stone and brick. Immediately through the bridge the remains of a concrete grit box are on the right. On the left a crude wooden platform, Park Leaze Halt, was built in 1960 as part of the railbus trial. No trace of it remains. Clamber up the rutted path beside the left hand abutment once through the bridge. Turn right along the lane carried by the bridge. Over the field on the right is a dense wood known as Railway Covert, so named for obvious reasons.

Follow the lane past a bungalow and a brick cottage on the left and cattle sheds on the right. Before reaching the Cotswold stone farm on the left the foot path turns right on the stone track just before the two oak trees in the hedge. Follow the stone track through and then left behind the wood in front until the T junction with another stone track, some three quarters of a mile. Turn right on this stone track towards the double line of pylons.

Cirencester Branch, Over The Severn Thames Canal

At the lowest point before the ground starts to rise to the pylons the path turns right along the field headland with the deep ditch and hedge on the left. There is a tall green footpath signpost for this right turn but no stile. Follow the ditch and hedge to the corner of the field then cross the wooden stile between the half dozen tatty pine trees. Once in the next field follow the headland clockwise beside the substantial railway embankment of the Cirencester branch then cross the wooden stile in the field corner between two more tatty pines and turn left on the tarmac lane through the brick underbridge. It is in fair condition although little more than a viaduct to carry afforestation over the lane. Half left and rising rather oddly out of the permanent pasture is another embankment. It carried the Severn Thames canal. Follow the lane as it rises onto this embankment and turn right through the gate opposite the stone cottage. The path now runs parrallel with the pylons on the right towards the hedge across the field. The foot path signpost at the gate has been turned round and should be ignored. The distinct depression in the field between path and pylons is the remains of the reinstated canal. Cross the high wooden stile in the hedge and turn right to follow the lane. The canal can be seen in a deep cutting parallel to the lane where the wood on the right comes to the very edge of the road. Even in the driest summers it holds a navigable depth of water just here. Take the first right up the lane signed as 'No Through', cross the now infilled canal overbridge then the railway overbridge at Park Leaze Halt, rejoin the line and follow it back to the parking place.

THE MALMESBURY BRANCH LINE
(Malmesbury, Wiltshire)

Ordnance Survey Map Sheet Explorer 168
Distance 4 and a quarter miles

Leave Malmesbury on the B4042 road for Swindon and take the first right, about 2 miles distant, signed The Somerfords. Travel downhill into Little Somerford and take the first right,just past the Saladin Inn, signed Great Somerford. Passing St John the Baptist's Church on the right a large railway underbridge appears. Park on the wide stone area on the left before the bridge. It was the entrance to the now closed Little Somerford Station which was the Malmesbury Branch connecting point with the Swindon/Bristol/South Wales main line. The iron Great Western Railway (GWR) station entrance gate posts still stand and bear the inscription 'T.James Vulcan Foundry Cardiff 1902'. The main line is still in frequent use and will be in sight or sound throughout this walk. The GWR owned Malmesbury Branch was opened in 1877 and originally connected with the Swindon/Chippenham/Bath main line at Dauntsey, 3 miles south east of Little Somerford. It ran through an intermediate station at Great Somerford thence to Malmesbury. The Swindon/South Wales main line did not open until 1903. Although it offered Malmesbury much nearer access to a main line the branch was not connected to it until 1933 at which time the remainder of the line to Dauntsey was closed. In the heyday of the Malmesbury branch annual statistics showed over 17,000 tickets sold and 16,700 tons of freight carried. It closed to passengers as early as 1951 but remained in use for freight only until 1962.

Follow Mill Lane opposite the parking place which runs parallel to the main line. Where the lane curves right there is a pond behind the hedge in the field on the left. The 1933 branch diverged from the main line just beyond the pond. Visible over the gate into the field is the wooden post and plain wire boundary fence of the branch which ran in a now reinstated cutting beyond the fence. At the highest point of the field is a wire straining post made of worn out rails. Note the fine viaduct carrying the main line westward over the River Avon. Stay on Mill Lane turning sharp left and going down hill. At the foot of the hill the branch line crossed Mill Lane. To the right is the Kingsmead level crossing keeper's cottage. Over the iron gate on the left the merging point of the 1877 and 1933 lines is clear. The 1877 line passed under the main Swindon/South Wales line. This was a very busy level crossing because it was on the only route in and out of Kingsmead Mill, a major supplier of animal fodder at the time. Turn right onto the track bed in front of the cottage and follow it through the wooden gate onto the embankment. The sign 'Private Property SFA' refers only to the parking spaces for those fishing in the Avon. The track curves left over a brick and concrete culvert. It is evidence of the well recorded difficulty that flooding caused while the line was in use. The rumour of a summer shower is still sufficient to inundate the field on the right just here. The curve ends at an iron gate followed immediately by a farm occupation level crossing. The crossing gate on the left has wire straining posts on either side made of old rails. Turn right here. The public path runs straight to the farm itself, Maunditts Park, up the hill through the wooden gate. Cross the cattle grid into the farm complex then another out of it and note the telegraph poles at the right of the farm drive. At the third one turn right to the iron gate across the field, go through it and cross the next field to the wooden gate. Cross the stile beside it and set off in the direction shown by the yellow arrow. As the field descends an iron gate appears in the hedge. Go through it, turn right then go through the gate immediately to the front. Continue down hill with the post and rail fence, ditch and thorn hedge at your left hand. At the foot of the hill go through the wicket gate in the hedge and cross the permanent pasture to the thatched red brick and timber cottage beside the road. Turn left through the village which is an uneasy mixture of beautiful old and starkly utilitarian new buildings. Bear right at the 'T' junction and keep right to pass through the main line underbridge. Immediately after the bridge turn right at the green public path sign post,cross the first field to the far right hand corner and cross the second field to the far right hand corner. Once over the wooden stile take the gate on the right into the ridge and furrow permanent pasture and make for the far right hand corner of that field as well. Go through the gate there and make for the bank of the River Avon on the left. Turn right and follow the bank as it meanders to the brick and local stone abutment of a bridge over the Avon on the 1877 branch line. An embankment runs right handed from the abutment on which is a Second War pill box. The line was by then disused so the pill box sits in the centre of the track. It formed part of the defences intended to prevent German invaders reaching Bristol.

Continue along the river bank, cross the stile onto the road and turn right. The house on the left was Great Somerford station on the 1877 line. Between it and the embankment on the right was a level crossing over the road. Continue along the road towards Little Somerford and mount the raised causeway on the left hand side where it has a wooden plank bed. It offers a clear view of the branch embankment continuing towards the 1903 Avon viaduct and Kingsmead. After leaf fall a farm occupation brick and concrete underbridge through the embankment is visible at the far side of the field. Rejoin the road and return to the parking place through the main line underbridge.

Bent Rail Straining Post, Malmesbury Branch

Avon Bridge Abutment, Malmesbury Branch

THE TETBURY BRANCH LINE
(Tetbury, Gloucestershire)

Ordnance Survey Map Sheet Explorer 168
Distance 3 and a half miles

Enter Tetbury on the B4067 'Cirencester Road' from the junction with the A433 road to the west of the town. As the built up area thickens on both sides the road descends through a single track section with the Royal Oak Inn on the left at the foot of the hill. Immediately past the Royal Oak enter the signed Old Station Car Park on the left through the white gates and park.

Tetbury Market House, built in 1650 and restored in the 1800's

The iron gate posts are original Great Western Railway (GWR), similar to those at Little Somerford. At one end of the car park the brick goods shed survives in fair condition. Behind it the cattle loading pens are to be seen. The public garden area over the stream on the 'Goods In' side of the shed used to be the cattle market which was built to take advantage of the railway. There are various plans to restore the goods shed and put it to use. The vertical Cotswold stone cliff dominating the site was cut for stone to raise the surface of the station area which was a water meadow. This also increased the size of the goods yard, now the car park. The GWR Tetbury Branch opened in 1889 and ran to Kemble where it connected with the Gloucester/Swindon main line and the Cirencester Branch. There was an intermediate station at Culkerton and halts for Rodmarton village and Kemble Aerodrome. In the early 1920's the line was carrying some 3,000 passengers, 13,800 tons of freight along with 436,000 gallons of milk and 300 wagon loads of livestock each year. However, by the early 1950's the 'Tetbury Flyer' as it was known was very underused. My brother and I travelled on it with our Nanny on occasional Monday afternoons at that period, changing at Kemble for Cirencester to buy fruit at the street market. Frequently we were the only passengers in the carriage. The line was closed in 1964 after an experimental diesel railbus service was introduced in 1959 which also ran on the Cirencester Branch.

The walk begins on the track bed at the end of the car park most distant from the goods shed. Although the line is now well wooded the fencing on both sides with bent rail straining posts, tapered concrete, old sleeper and old rail uprights is unmistakeable evidence that it was a railway. To the left side is an unusual profusion of old rail uprights. Being narrow and heavy much more work was required to set them firm and vertical. After a straight section the line curves gently left on an embankment through which a well made brick culvert carries the Tetbury branch of the River Avon. The river flow is from right to left. Another culvert appears shortly to carry a meander of the river from left to right. The line enters a cutting through which there is a public footpath occupation crossing. In 1891 an elderly and deaf farm worker was run over and killed on the crossing by the 5.20 afternoon train from Kemble. Go through the hunt gate in the wooden fence across the line and continue along the embankment. Immediately after the gate is a third culvert, in very good condition, with a flow from right to left. The line curves right handed into a minor cutting then onto an embankment over which there is a gated farm occupation level crossing. On the right are 8 tubular concrete anti tank bollards. They were positioned to anchor obstacles across the line and block it to tanks and other vehicles in 1940.

They were part of a defence line intended to prevent invading German forces from reaching Bristol. The line now curves left and enters a cutting. Atop the bank on the left at the highest point are two thick, cemented Cotswold stone wall ends. They were part of the same defence work and mark a gap in a deep ditch, known as a tank trap, dug to hinder battle tank movement. The gap was for the railway line. Continue on to a modest embankment where another culvert carries the stream from left to right. A steep grass bank then blocks the track. It marks the position of a brick and steel girder overbridge sadly demolished and infilled to cope with modern lorry weights. Turn sharp right up the stone path between the thorn bushes to the hunt gate into the lane. Turn right again uphill and note that the fence either side of the road in the final approach to the bridge is the original railway supply. From the lane at the top of the hill, Lark Hill, the course of the branch is shown by the woods lining the valley bottom right back to Tetbury which is marked by the spire of St Mary's church.

The distance to cover on the lane is exactly one mile. From Lark Hill it dips to a cross lanes then rises between farm cottages and past another defence work, a red brick pill box, on the right. Soon after the pill box there are field gates exactly opposite each other on either side of the lane and a dark green foot path sign at a wooden stile in the hedge on the right. Cross the stile and follow the headland round the pond and along the wall to the next stile in a hedge. On a line between this stile and the spire of St Mary's church is a gate in the far right hand corner of the next field. Go through it and make for the radio mast beside the barns at the far right hand corner of the next field. Enter the farm yard and follow the concrete track left handed between the buildings. Stay on the concrete track until a stone stile and a metal kissing gate are on the right directly under a crossing overhead electric line. Enter the field over the stile and through the kissing gate then follow the headland clockwise down hill. Ahead and half right the complex roof scape of old Tetbury shows up well. At the field corner go through the kissing gate and turn right down hill along the pavement beside the main road. At the foot of the hill between two more GWR gate posts on the right is the southern entrance to Tetbury station. Enter the gateway. The lane leads back to the goods shed and car park. The passenger station, in final form an elegant little Edwardian brick building completed in 1916, was about half way to the goods shed. Nothing whatever remains of it.

Cattle Loading Pens, Tetbury Station

THE MARLBOROUGH BRANCH LINE
(Marlborough, Wiltshire)

Ordnance Survey Map Sheet Explorer 157
Distance 5 and three quarter miles

Take the A346 road south from Marlborough towards Salisbury. After a mile and a half the road passes through the hamlet of Cadley. Take the first right after Cadley, about a mile,which is a lane signed to Wotton Rivers and Brimslade. After a further half mile the lane, Hat Gate Lane,turns sharp left through ninety degrees. Park on the broad grass verge on the right just as the bend begins. Take the lane down hill from the parking place between the abutments of two consecutive railway underbridges. The first carried the double line of the Midland & South Western Junction Railway (MSWJR) and the second the Marlborough Branch Line.

The bricks on the MSWJR bridge are visibly flaking away but they are in good condition on the other which was built 20 years earlier.

The Marlborough Branch was opened in 1864 and connected the town with the Great Western Railway (GWR) owned London/Newbury/Westbury main line at a station called Savernake, some 2 miles south east of Hat Gate Lane. There were no intermediate stations on the 5 and a half mile line. The branch was operated by the GWR but construction was financed by local entrepreneurs gathered in the Marlborough Railway Company (MRC). This company retained a profitable ownership of the branch until 1896 when it sold out to the GWR, which, as it transpired,was at just the right moment. In 1883 the Swindon, Marlborough and Andover Railway Company (SMA) had opened a line from Swindon to Marlborough and from Andover to Savernake and had statutory running rights over the Marlborough Branch to connect the three towns in the company name. This generated extra traffic for the branch and dividends for MRC share holders. However the GWR, routinely jealous of rival railway companies, never delivered efficient access to SMA trains arriving at either end of the branch. Therefore, in 1898, the MSWJR, who now owned the SMA, opened a line from Marlborough to Savernake which was entirely their own making them independent of the GWR, hence the proximity of the Hat Gate Lane bridges. At a stroke the Marlborough Branch was left serving a town which was on the MSWJR main line. Use and profits slumped accordingly with annual ticket sales down from 20,000 to 5,000. In 1924 the MSWJR was absorbed by the GWR but it was not until 1933 that the branch was closed, the track lifted and the lines merged, at a point passed during this walk. All rail traffic ceased between Savernake and Marlborough in 1966.

Just past the second Hat Gate Lane underbridge take the bridle path on the right indicated by the pony sign. Known as Mud Lane it runs beside both branch and MSWJR lines which are the heavily wooded embankments on the right. Some 150 yards from the pony sign the 1933 merging of the lines takes place. It is a thorny task to see the actual spot but can be done. When the thicket ends the point where the branch was reinstated to farm land is marked by wire strained on recycled rails. The MSWJR line curves away right handed and takes a direct route to Marlborough parallel with the A346. Continue on Mud Lane past a well signed crossing foot path to a gently rising left curve. On the right is a wrecked wooden gate with a yellow foot path arrow on the hanging post. Go through the gate and follow the right hand side of the hedge and tree belt immediately in front. When this ends continue down hill following the right side of the mixed sheep netting and barbed wire fence. Already visible is a section of Marlborough Branch embankment which perfectly illustrates the function of such engineering. It joins by a level route two minor crests at either side of a valley. A charming key hole shaped farm and foot path occupation underbridge is at the centre of the embankment. It is made of brick and local Marlborough Downs Sarsen stone and is in very fair condition although both parapets are cracked. Go through the bridge, turn left and walk parallel with the line up hill to a small plantation of mixed oak, ash and conifers which bulges out into the field. Turn left on to the branch line immediately after the plantation then right handed along the track way. It runs straight into a slight cutting which glitters with dense clumps of snow drops in January and February.

Keyhole Bridge, Marlborough Branch

Next there is a farm and foot path level crossing marked by wire straining posts made with recycled rails and more rails with hinges attached on which to hang crossing gates. Stay on the line which continues straight through another shallow cutting then onto a tall, narrow embankment. As the embankment begins to diminish it is crossed by a well marked foot path. The original and unusual stiles made of upright rails joined by round steel rods provide access onto and off the track. Given the steep embankment it is surprising that an underbridge was not provided. It may be that because the line ran along an existing and still current farm boundary there was no need to provide field to field horse and cart routes for a single land owner. The peasants on Shank's Pony could perfectly well scramble over the railway. Cross the stile on the right of the embankment, turn half left and follow the grass strip uphill from tree to tree right into the corner of the field where there is an in and out wooden post and rail hunt jump. The branch line continues behind the wood on the left beginning the descent to Marlborough in a deepening cutting.

Cross the hunt jump, make for the tall circular post with blue right of way arrows straight ahead then turn right along the head land with the barbed wire on your left hand. At the next field corner go through the gap in the rough bank covered in oak trees. The bank is Wansdyke which is a pre-Roman linear defence work. Go straight across the next field and when the power cables are overhead aim to be equidistant from the cable pole on Wansdyke and that to it's left at which point a field gate will be visible in the hedge to the front. Go through the gate and follow the grass strip on your left down hill beside the line of sweet chestnut trees. There are loose Sarsen stones beside the strip which have been cleared from the fields. At the next field corner is a conifer wood. Enter it and follow the stone track right handed then turn left at the tarmac lane. It passes through an embankment of the MSWJR Savernake to Marlborough section. The underbridge has been dismantled and removed. The line ran left handed towards Marlborough into a very deep cutting and a tunnel of some 650 yards and right handed to Savernake. As the lane curves sharp left after the embankment cross the wooden stile on the right marked by the yellow arrow. Follow the field head land clockwise with the major embankment and a host of Sarsen stones to the right. Cross the post and rail stile where the wire ends and the hedge begins then turn right up hill beside the hedge. Continue to follow the hedge closely which itself turns right. The MSWJR is to the front in a cutting crossed by a brick and steel farm occupation overbridge which is now a bridge for the hedge. Turn left and follow the field headland parallel with the line. As the ground descends the embankment for the railway becomes higher. There is then a farm and footpath occupation underbridge. It is a strictly utilitarian brick and steel construction unlike the keyhole occupation underbridge on the branch line. Continue beside the line to the stone track and turn right through the embankment. Here again the underbridge has been dismantled and removed. Stay on the stone track which rises gently to the farm and foot path level crossing previously encountered on the branch line. Now take the route used from Hat Gate Lane to return there.

THE TIDWORTH BRANCH LINE
(Tidworth, Wiltshire)

Ordnance Survey Map Sheet Explorer 131
Distance 5 and a half miles

Take the A346 road signed to Andover and Ludgershall,where it leaves the A338 Marlborough to Salisbury road at Collingbourne Ducis. At the crest of Shaw Hill reached after one mile take the well signed left turn to Wexcombe. After some 300 yards there is an infilled hump back bridge over the Midland & South Western Junction Railway (MSWJR) line between Ludgershall and Marlborough where there are double metal gates on the right hand side. Park in the gateway, which is redundant,and descend onto the line, which runs through a modest cutting, via the stile to the left of the double gates. The track bed here is a public Conservation Walk sponsored by the Ministry of Agriculture which offers a fine show of cowslips and field scabious in their seasons. Follow the line. The cutting shallows to a farm occupation level crossing where the railway supplied gate hanging and wire straining posts are still extant. The line now enters a second cutting which in turn shallows to another farm level crossing where there are more original gate posts. This is followed by an embankment with earth parapets rising about a foot above the track bed. They may have been to control water run off and prevent erosion of the chalk soil in the embankment. The line curves left to a dilapidated farm occupation underbridge from which most of the parapets have fallen onto the verge of the track below. Curiously the buttresses on the west side are all brick while those on the east are local stone. There is now another cutting at the deepest point of which there are the remains of an occupation overbridge consisting of brick and local stone abutments while the span appears to be the rubble scattered on the track. The cutting ends at the A342 road which used to pass over the railway. The remains of this overbridge are in the undergrowth on the left hand as the line reaches the main road. Turn left along the wide verge of the road and take the first right into Hei-Lin Way, go past the children's playground on the right and into Williamson Close. Go straight through the close on the tarmac foot path, signed by a walking man symbol, with the Church of St James on the left hand. Take the steep steps up to the road and turn right onto the new bridge carrying the A3026 over the now intact railway.

To the left is the original Victorian overbridge and the railway leading off to a junction with the London to Salisbury to Southampton main line some 5 miles away. To the right is the training centre for Royal Engineer railway repair teams. It was the goods yard of the MSWJR Ludgershall station. To the left of the various sidings and platforms in the training centre a single line curves away left handed into the trees. It is the Tidworth Branch. The branch was built by the War Department and opened in 1901 to initially transport building materials from Ludgershall station to Tidworth Camp, then under construction, thereafter to carry men and equipment to the camp for manoeuvres on Salisbury Plain. There were no intermediate stations. In 1903 the branch was leased to the MSWJR to be operated and maintained for public and military use. The military use was so intense that before the Great War the 2 and a half mile branch was producing more annual revenue than all the other stations on the MSWJR put together. It closed to public use and reverted to War Department operation in 1955. In 1961 the branch was closed entirely.

Continue over the new bridge and follow the pavement on the right side of the main road past Corunna Barracks on the left with the well preserved Centurion tank adapted for Royal Engineer use at the gate. The branch continues through the trees on the far side of the arable field on the right. visible is an original gated farm level crossing now redundant since it is within a secure area. As the ground rises a siding leads away from the branch across the A3026 and into the barracks on the far side. Immediately after this level crossing the Castledown School and public playing fields are on the right. Enter them from the bus request stop, turn right and follow the perimeter fence. The whole sports area is on two levels divided by a line of sycamore trees. By following the perimeter fence this line is reached where, behind the trees on the right, are the buffers at the end of what is left of the Tidworth Branch. It is decorated with a 'Tanks Keep Out' sign. Continue along

the edge of the playing fields to the next corner where there is a gap in the fence between two more sycamores. Go through the gap and turn left on the tarmac lane. At the T junction turn left down hill then take the stone track beside the farm buildings, first right. There was a branch underbridge just below this point. All that remains are raised concrete verges on either side of the lane. They were put up in the 1930's to protect the abutments of the bridge from battle tanks slewing round the corner and crashing into the brick work. To the left of the stone track a low embankment is visible in the undergrowth. When the track veers right into the farm yard turn left onto

The End of the Line, Tidworth Branch   the embankment then right on the track bed. It ends at a concrete tank road. Turn right up hill on the tank road which curves gently left to the crest then descends past a deciduous plantation. The branch ran in a spectacular, almost vertical, bright white chalk cutting which has sadly been reinstated and is beneath this plantation. At the foot of the hill turn left off the road and follow the wire fence enclosing the plantation towards the over head power cables. Once under the cables turn right down the narrow path between the blackthorn bushes. It is the start of what becomes a very tall, narrow and heavily wooded embankment which carried the line right into North Tidworth. The path emerges at the A3026 where the underbridge has been completely removed.

Descend from the embankment on the chalk path and turn sharp right on the chalk track which runs parallel to the line then curves back under the power cables and running beside a very thick hedge on the left returns to the tank road. Go straight across the road and continue on the chalk track, now deeply rutted and rising,with another thick hedge at the left side. It reaches a fork,now among scrub on the steep hill side. Take the left. A 'T' junction follows shortly. Again take the left. The track soon begins to descend towards a mixed pine and beech strip wood. Turn left on the far side of this wood on another chalk track leading down hill to a 'T' junction with yet another chalk track. Turn right at this junction and make for the the dairy complex at Sunnyhill Farm. The public right of way skirts the right side of the farm buildings and emerges on the A342 road. Go straight across the road and up the stone track which leads back to the crest of Shaw Hill and the turning to the Wexcombe lane parking place.

Start of the Line, Tidworth Branch

THE NAILSWORTH BRANCH LINE
(near Stroud, Gloucestershire)

Ordnance Survey Map Sheet Explorer 168
Distance 8 and a quarter miles

Enter Nailsworth on the A46 road from Stroud. Just before the roundabout at the centre of Nailsworth take the left turn at the sign for Egypt Mill. Take the next left opposite the Railway Hotel, now converted to flats, and passing the Fire Brigade compound on the right enter the large gravel and tarmac car park.

The Station, Nailsworth Branch

It was the goods yard of Nailsworth Station. The first sod for the Stonehouse and Nailsworth Railway Company (SNR) was cut in 1864 and the line was open in 1867, operated by the Midland Railway Company (MR). The branch ran from the MR main line at Stonehouse through intermediate stations at Ryeford, Dudbridge and Woodchester to Nailsworth. In 1885 a sub - branch from Dudbridge to Stroud was added although Stroud was already served by a Great Western Railway (GWR) main line. In 1886 the SNR was absorbed by the MR. Nailsworth lies in a valley which results from a bifurcation of the Golden Valley containing Stroud. The Golden Valley is so named because it has been home to successful industries from Mediaeval times. The Nailsworth valley was just as successful an industrial area hence the need for a railway line. Products from works along the line and carried as freight on it included cloth, timber, paper, dye, engineering equipment, arms and munitions, furniture, bedding, as well as human and animal food stuffs. A number of manufacturers had private sidings on the line. Using 1912 as an example year individual tickets sold on the branch numbered 143,994 while

103,785 tons of freight were shifted, so the tons came quite close to the tickets. In the post Great War railway reorganisation the MR became the London Midland and Scottish Railway (LM&SR). The passenger service was withdrawn in 1947 and the branch closed entirely in 1966. Lengths of it are now surfaced and designated as a bicycle and foot path.

Go through the five bar gate at the far end of the car park (goods yard). The wooded embankment on the right carried the passenger trains on their final approach to the station which still stands on the platform beside the track bed. Happily the station, now a private home, is in excellent condition and unspoilt by extensions or improvements. It is well worth scrambling up the embankment to have a look at it. The householder is understanding about interest in the building. Shortly the goods and passenger lines merge and continue as one along an embankment beside the Nailsworth Stream on the left. Then on the left behind a stout post and rail fence are stone and red brick cloth mills converted to flats. On the right at this point is a plain tubular steel hand rail beside steps leading down to a brick and stone foot path occupation underbridge. Headroom beneath it is very limited. The bridge parapets beside the line are overgrown but intact. Fifty paces beyond the right hand parapet beneath the tapered concrete post and plain wire railway fence is an MR boundary marker. Some two feet high it is like a solid steel spoon stuck in the ground by the handle with the MR inscribed on the far side. The next item of interest is an all brick farm occupation underbridge in apparently good condition but with one abutment reinforced with new concrete clocks. The bridge no longer leads anywhere because while to the right is still farm land to the left is a secure industrial site.

The industrial site continues behind a mesh fence on the left. The track bed has been covered in tarmac on this section. The mesh then gives way to a solid steel spike high security fence and the path narrows considerably at an underbridge made with a hotch potch of local stone, steel, timber brick and concrete. It can be explored via the yellow arrowed foot path stile on the right. The original LM&SR wrought iron and wood decorative gates to close the lane beneath the bridge are still on their hinges. The open area on the left was one of the private sidings already

Footpath underbridge, Nailsworth Branch

- 27 -

mentioned. The line now descends perceptibly beneath a concrete 1950's replacement overbridge with the original brick abutment on the left side. The bridge bears a narrow lane with the original 20 Ton limit signs in place.

Where the security fence ends the track returns to full width and enters a cutting. Shortly after there is a foot path level crossing with an original sleeper foot bridge over the drain at the base of the gently sloping approach on the right side. The cutting deepens rapidly and the track curves right beneath the 1960's concrete overbridge presently carrying the A46 road then the redundant brick and steel overbridge which used to carry the A46. The contrast between the strict utility of the first and the delicate inner vaulting of the second is striking. The line now runs close to the Nailsworth Stream and past a chemical industry compound on the right which was the site of Woodchester Station. At the far end of the compound is the Station Master's red brick house, now a private residence. Here there was a level crossing over Woodchester Lane followed shortly by another over a lane leading to St Mary's Church, Woodchester. The line then curves left over a crude metal bridge set at an oblique angle across and just above the Nailsworth Stream which from now on runs on the right hand. Immediately after the bridge there was a deep cutting which is now infilled and covered with housing. However, the well marked public path runs between the houses, over a road which did not exist when the branch was in use then back into the remaining section of the cutting and under a brick and steel overbridge bearing the lane to North Woodchester. The bridge has been reinforced with steel sympathetic to the original design which is identical to the 19th Century A46 bridge. As soon as the cutting ends the line meanders through a long right hand then left hand curve on an embankment sloping more or less steeply down to the Nailsworth Stream on the right. There is a sharp dip in the track where an underbridge has been removed which gave passage to a foot path. Next there is a handsome brick underbridge in good condition whose function has disappeared, seemingly due to soil and rubbish tipping. On the right it gives access to the private water garden of a handsome Cotswold stone house and to the left an elder wood on a rough bank reaches right up to the arch. A stream does run through it but this bridge is much more than a culvert.

The scene to the right now becomes increasingly industrial which is appropriate to the reasons for the foundation of the branch. As these factories then give way to a recent housing development a modern steel sculpture sign post modelled on a giant bicycle chain appears on the track bed. By chance it marks the spot where the Stroud Branch joined the Nailsworth Branch. To left and right are brick walls which mark the close approach to what was Dudbridge Station of which nothing else remains. Obeying the frequent blue and white bicycle symbols turn right at the sculpture signpost and take the tarmac path through the housing estate, crossing the Nailsworth Stream and reaching the main road.

Cross the road and climb the flight of concrete steps to regain the track bed of the Stroud Branch. It is at this height above the road because the line ran from Dudbridge Station through what is now the housing estate on a substantial embankment, since removed, to an underbridge for the road, then designated the A4096. The course of bricks to the left side of the concrete steps are all that remains of this bridge. Follow the line which passes almost immediately beneath a steel and brick overbridge carrying Dudbridge Hill Road then curves persistently right handed round the foot of the Rodborough/Minchinhampton Common feature. This towers between and separates the Golden Valley and Nailsworth Valley. The line then straightens onto an embankment with a deep drop on the left. Visible in quick succession on the left are thick and thin upright cast iron capstans on concrete bases then a circular concrete pit with a lip on the track side. On the opposite side of the pit a series of tall concrete steps stretch down to the foot of the embankment. All these are the remains of a siding from which coal was unloaded by an ingenious system of winches and a hydraulic ram which upended whole wagons so tipping their contents down a chute for use by the Stroud Gas Works. The line then continues into a cutting and in rapid succession beneath two overbridges. The first bears the A46 and is constructed of brick and steel, it has some features in common with the A46 overbridge near Woodchester. The second is all brick with a stepped parapet and bears Rodborough Hill Road. Soon after this bridge the gravel track bed surface comes to an end. Here turn left off the line and ascend the tarmac path to Rodborough Hill Road then turn right and follow the pavement to the foot of the hill where there is a road bridge over the River Frome. Bear right over the area of modern cobble stones towards the pedestrian underpass then sharp right at the Saint John's Ambulance Brigade building to reach the bank of the River Frome. On the far side are the six remaining brick arches of the Wallbridge viaduct which carried the branch over the Frome and into Stroud Station, Midland Railway. The Stroud Branch was a bare 1 and a quarter miles long but even from what remains it can be seen that a major engineering effort was required to construct it. However, it seems the investment was well judged and the line was profitable despite the proximity of the GWR main line station. The latter is still in use. Follow the Frome upstream by climbing the steps beside the concrete road retaining wall. This road did not exist when the railway functioned and is built over most of the area of the station. From the metal barrier at the verge half way up the steps part of what was the goods area is visible across the road, now a light industrial/retail yard. Climb to the top of the steps, cross the wooden stile, descend to the river bank and continue upstream. Note that the duck board path rests on a sleeper base and the embankment of the new road on the left is studded with wood, concrete, brick and steel railway scrap.

Cross the Frome on the foot bridge beneath the fine GWR viaduct, take the tarmac drive leading up from the river and where it veers left turn sharp right through the metal kissing gate into the permanent pasture. Incline slightly left towards the prominent lone oak tree and from it make for the hedge which separates the field from the housing estate on the right. Follow the hedge up hill and at the field corner go through an identical kissing gate into the ash wood, follow the well beaten path between the trees, still up hill, through another identical kissing gate and up the wooden steps to the foot ball field. Climb the stone steps in front of the club house to the car park at the right of the building.

Cross the lane at the car park exit, go through the white painted wicket gate onto the tarmac public foot path and follow it to the next white wicket gate which opens onto Rodborough Hill Road. Cross this road taking the sign posted lane to Little London,not to Tabernacle Walk. On the high ground to the left is the Victorian Gothic style Rodborough Fort which was used to store works of art from London galleries during the Blitz in the Second War. To the right is a panoramic view of the Nailsworth valley with the course of the branch line and the industrial sites it served clearly visible. Stay on the lane to Little London as it ascends then descends through mixed conifer and beech woods then turn right, steeply downhill over the cattle grid on Bowl Hill Road. Turn left on Rooksmoor Hill and descend to the A46 road. Go straight across it, turn left on the pavement then right at the first telegraph pole encountered and down to the concrete foot bridge over the Rooksmoor Mill weir. At the mill turn left and follow the paved walkway beside the wall which becomes a dirt and cinders track up the embankment of the Nailsworth Branch. Turn left on the track to return to the parking place.

Midland Railway Gates, Nailsworth Branch

THE CALNE BRANCH LINE
(near Chippenham, Wiltshire)

Ordnance Survey Map Sheet Explorer 156
Distance 4 and a half miles

Take the A4 main road from Chippenham to Calne and Marlborough. About a mile west of Chippenham at the foot of Derry Hill there is a junction with the A432 road. Stay on the A4 climbing Derry Hill and at the crest turn left into Studley Lane signed to Stanley. Take the first left, again signed to Stanley, and the next left down a steep hill on a single track lane. At the foot of the hill the verges widen on either side and after half a mile there is a modest hump in the lane followed immediately by a gravel car park on the right marked by a large, blue, solid steel national cycle way sign post. Park here and follow the gravel path up the bank at the other side of the car park then turn right on an embankment of the Calne Branch Line.

The branch, built by the Calne Railway Company (CRC) and worked by the Great Western Railway (GWR) opened in October 1863. Some 5 and a half miles of single track it ran from the GWR main line at Chippenham through two intermediate halts at Stanley Bridge and Black Dog to the terminus in Calne. Calne was home of the Harris family bacon factory, the biggest bacon business in Great Britain then, and although the town had been served by a branch from the Wiltshire & Berkshire Canal since September 1810 this could not carry the sheer bulk of pigs in and bacon out. The GWR bought out the CRC in June 1892. By 1900 it was routinely possible to travel by train from Calne to Paddinton in precisely two hours. The branch continued to flourish into the Twentieth Century carrying Harris freight along with personnel and supplies for two major Royal Air Force bases opened in 1935 at Compton Bassett and Yatesbury, just east of Calne. As late as 1953 over 300,000 passengers and some 10,000 wagons of freight travelled the line turning over £150,000. A prolonged national railway workers strike in 1955 forced most of this traffic onto the roads. The branch was closed to freight in 1963 and to passengers in 1965.

Go through the wicket gate on the embankment. At once to left and right a deep but heavily overgrown cut runs right up to the embankment. It is the Wiltshire and Berkshire Canal which ran from Melksham to Abingdon and passed through the embankment via a local stone underbridge. The hump just before the car park is the remains of a bridge which carried the lane over the canal. The canal closed in 1914 and the bridge under the railway line was infilled and reinforced in 1934. Follow the branch into a cutting with thick hawthorn bushes to each side. In the blossom season this section is like a bright white scented tunnel. The line curves slightly left handed beneath a keyhole occupation overbridge for Stanley Abbey Farm made of local stone in excellent condition. Note the sole surviving railway telegraph pole complete with insulators just beyond this bridge on the right hand side.

The cutting shallows to the level and the odd original railway fence post appears on the right, both tapered concrete and recycled sleepers. The track bed now runs straight along a minor embankment in which there is an infilled brick and stone farm occupation underbridge and a culvert of the same materials. Beside the parapet of the bridge on the left a black, lagged six inch pipe runs on the surface. It carried water from a private bore hole along the branch to the Harris factory in Calne. The bacon curing process demanded much more water than the town supply could provide so the pipe was laid in 1932 and surfaces at each underbridge. The track then curves right handed into a thick wood and the embankment becomes steeper. The original GWR boundary fence survives at the base of the embankment on both sides, on the right is a wire straining post made from a recycled rail. At a level point half way through the wood there is a farm occupation crossing followed by a cutting spanned by a road overbridge similar to that at Stanley Abbey Farm but with a brick lining to the inner arch which has recently been repaired. The track now straightens along a narrow, rising embankment. There is then a farm occupation underbridge with a steel span and stone abutments. It is an extraordinarily wide span for farm access in the 1860's, well suited to the largest present day machinery. Perhaps the steel work was second hand or a standard length rather than made to order. Note the lagged Harris water pipe on the surface by the left parapet. The embankment, now lessening, again enters woodland with original GWR fencing on the right then emerges into more open country. At this point cross the style beside the hunt gate in the fence on the left and take the well beaten path downhill to the metal gate at the opposite side of the permanent pasture. The branch line continues right handed over the A4 road on a new bridge built for bicycles. To the left the Harris water pipe is visible above ground, diverted from the line to a modern sewage works.

Cross the wooden stile on the right side of the metal gate and follow the stone track on the hump back bridge over the River Marden and left handed to the tarmac lane. Turn right then immediately left over the wooden stile in the hedge. On the top of the stile is a yellow foot path arrow pointing at a power cable pole in the field. Make for this pole and cross another wooden stile between it and another metal gate. Turn right and follow the field headland uphill, through a final gate/stile combination and continue uphill to a tarmac lane where there is a prominent metal sign with a walking man symbol. Turn left downhill on the lane, cross the brook and climb steeply past the thatched cottages on the right. The lane then runs on the level to the foot of the next hill where there is a gravel drive to Hazeland Farm on the left and an open area of concrete on the right. Turn left into Hazeland Farm.

At the end of the drive the foot path forks left into the concrete farm yard then right in front of the long, low tin roofed barn, up the grass bank then left again on the grass track which has wire sheep net fencing on both sides. Follow the grass track through the heavy metal gate then turn left downhill on the tarmac lane. There is a triangular sign on the left verge warning of a sharp left bend. Stand beside the sign and look left along the deep cut and line of alder trees at the headland of the field. They mark the course of the Calne branch of the Wiltshire & Berkshire Canal. The railway branch runs along a similar contour but on the opposite side of the valley. Continue downhill on the lane, crossing the bridge over the weir then rising to the branch line overbridge.

To the right is a North Wiltshire County Council nature trail sign at the top of a flight of stone steps leading down to the track bed. Turn right on the track and return to the parking place.

Stanley Abbey Bridge, Calne Branch

THE HIGHWORTH BRANCH LINE
(near Swindon, Wiltshire)

Ordnance Survey Map Sheet Explorer 169
Distance 2 and a half miles

Take the A419 road from Cirencester to Swindon. The final approach to the latter is up the steep Blunsdon Hill into a 50 MPH speed limit. At the top of the hill are traffic lights and shortly after them turn left, signed to Highworth, on the B4019 just before the Cold Harbour Hotel. The B4019 descends gently for the first two miles then crosses the Stanton Water Brook on a left hand bend via a bridge with brick parapets and metal crash barriers on each side. Immediately after the bridge there is a field entrance on the left which is shut by the the original level crossing wood and metal braced gate still hanging where it was used to close the B4019 to allow the Highworth Branch Line train to cross. In the hedge on the right side before the bridge the original level crossing approach fencing is still visible. Take the first right after the bridge, signed for Stanton Fitzwarren, and enter the village on Trenchard Road. On the right Mill Lane appears beside a small village green equipped with wooden benches beneath two silver birch trees. Park by the pavement on the left side of Trenchard Road. Walk down Mill Lane, named Station Lane between the 1860's and 1960's, cross again the Stanton Water Brook on the stone bridge and as the lane rises note the penultimate house on the right, Old Station House.

Level Crossing Gate, Highworth Branch

The central part of it,between the tall red brick chimneys,was home of the Stanton Fitzwarren Station head porter. The station was not big enough to warrant a master. The present householder is sympathetic to railway enthusiasm. The station,along with others at Stratton and Hannington, was intermediate between Swindon and Highworth on the 6 and a half mile branch line. The line opened in May 1883 and was an exclusively Great Western Railway (GWR) enterprise. The main line station was Swindon Town and the branch diverted north between the Lower Stratton and Gorse Hill areas of modern Swindon. At the time almost every acre between there and Highworth was rich dairy country and up to five trains a day in each direction carried milk, other agricultural produce and people along the branch. The passenger service was withdrawn in 1953 but the line continued in freight use until 1961. Surviving local memory is that the service was efficient and popular. The utility of the line now running through the sprawling dormitory suburbs of Swindon is manifest.

Where the tarmac of Mill Lane becomes stone, beside the last house on the right, was a level crossing at right angles to the line which ran left handed into the woods to Swindon and right handed to Highworth. On the left one of the original oak and steel crossing gates and the two shoulder height kissing gates for the foot path are still on their hinges in the undergrowth but easily visible, indeed the farthest kissing gate is in good working order. Stanton Station itself was on the Highworth side of the crossing. No trace of it remains. Follow the stone track until the corner of the wood on the left then turn left as indicated by the Wiltshire foot path sign to Kingsdown. The path, now with open fields on the right, continues beside the wood on the left to a gap in a thick hedge giving access to a permanent pasture. Follow the well beaten foot path to the far left hand corner of the pasture.

The branch line emerges from the wood to the left on a modest embankment which forms the enclosure along that side of the field. The embankment is revetted with a Cotswold stone wall to make it stock proof which is an unusually expensive alternative to the usual plain wire. There is a narrow steel and stone farm occupation underbridge through the embankment. The span of redundant sleepers is not original. The foot path rises to what was a farm occupation level crossing. The provision of two routes over/under the line from the same field to the same field on the same property within 100 yards of each other is unusual. There may have been more enclosures in different ownership during the Nineteenth Century. Turn right and follow the branch track bed along the embankment. At the foot of the embankment on the left sections of the usual post and wire fence survive. The footpath now descends righthanded from the embankment beside a dismantled underbridge of which the concrete and stone abutments survive. Continue along the farm track parallel with the embankment to the left which is still revetted with

Cotswold stone. The line itself is impenetrably wooded at this point. Watch for a lone sleeper set upright in the ground on the wide grass verge between the branch and the track. Twenty paces beyond it turn left through the gap in the bushes onto the branch which is now level with the farm track and turn immediately right into a deepening cutting with original railway fencing on both sides. The cutting is plenty wide enough for a double line compared with the embankment leading to it. The soil type here may have been vulnerable to erosion and slipping onto the tracks so not suitable for narrow cuttings. The cutting ends at a farm occupation level crossing with a modern concrete surface.

Follow the track bed into the wood, Great Wood, on a low embankment with original tapered concrete railway fence posts on both sides. Soon the jumbled remains of a brick and stone farm occupation overbridge which crossed the line at a very oblique angle are apparent. It is quite an elaborate bit of civil engineering with steep ramps well fenced with wire strained on recycled upright rails. An original wooden gate giving access from the right hand bridge approach to the railway still hangs. Given the lie of the land a level crossing would seem to have been good enough unless the use of this farm road, marked on early Twentieth Century maps as is Great Wood, was very frequent and included much livestock. Continue along the line onto another low embankment with a wide base to cope with the boggy ground through which it passes. This section of the walk ends where Kingsdown Lane bridle path crosses the branch via a level crossing. The original gate is still in place closing the line to trains from Swindon. At the keeper end a short length of rail protrudes from the ground.

Turn right on Kingsdown Lane passing a modern galvanised kissing gate and the beginning of the perimeter of Swindon Municipal Crematorium gardens on the left. As the ground starts to rise beside these gardens there is an angle iron and wood stile indicated by a yellow foot path arrow in the hedge on the right. Cross the stile and follow the headland clockwise to the first field corner. Go through the gap in the hedge there and follow the cart track beside Great Wood to the right. At the junction of the cart track and the concrete farm road re-enter the branch line cutting and return to the parking place on the route already walked.

GWR Kissing Gate, Highworth Branch

THE FAIRFORD BRANCH LINE
(near Lechlade, Gloucestershire)

Ordnance Survey Map Sheet Outdoor Leisure 45
Distance 5 and a half miles

Take the A417 road from Lechlade to Faringdon. Take the second left turning, the B4449 signed to Kelmscot and Bampton. Again take the second left turning, a single track lane signed to Little Faringdon and Bampton. Shortly there is a sharp double bend where the lane passes under a triple power cable and on the subsequent straight stretch there is a group of farm barns on the right and a stone lay by on the left. There is ample space in the lay by to park without obstructing the field gates at each end. This spot and the entire walk are within Oxfordshire. Continue on foot along the lane towards the Cotswold stone building visible ahead. It is called Crossing Cottage and was just that, the home of the Little Faringdon Lane level crossing keeper. Only the part of the house parallel with the lane is original, the rest is a modern but cleverly integrated extension. The stone tracks leading left to Lechlade and right to Witney off the lane just before Crossing Cottage follow the line of the Fairford Branch.

A branch line from Oxford to Witney was opened by the Witney Railway Company (WRC) in 1861. It was first operated by the West Midland Railway Company (WMRC) then, from 1863, by the Great Western Railway (GWR). Also in 1861 the East Gloucestershire Railway Company (EGRC) was formed with the intention of extending the Witney branch through to Cheltenham via Fairford so making it a main line. The line from Witney to Fairford was opened in 1873 and operated by the GWR but both the WRC and EGRC were soon bankrupt and their assets,including the 22 mile line from Oxford to Fairford, were eventually acquired outright by the GWR in 1890. The bankruptcy scuppered the plan to reach Cheltenham but the legacy of the EGRC was the 14 mile railway from Witney to Fairford. It passed through intermediate stations at Brize Norton, Carterton, Alvescot, Langford and Lechlade. The line ran through a world of villages with populations of 200 or 300, even Fairford and Lechlade were barely a quarter of their size today, so it is not surprising that passengers were not the staple of the branch. It was agricultural freight which made work for 4 to 6 trains per day for over 70 years. Routinely 800,000 gallons of milk were carried along the line each year on their journey to London. The peak of activity came in the Second War when unprecedented and unrepeated quantities of military material and personnel came down the branch to the major Royal Air Force airfields at Fairford, Brize Norton and Broadwell, the two former being still operational.

The post war decline in railway use bore down hard on the branch section Witney to Fairford and it was closed in 1962. The section Oxford to Witney, supported by the world famous Witney blanket industry survived until 1970.

Turn right onto the line following the green public birdleway sign. Only the tapered concrete fence posts in the hedge to the left reveal that it ever was a railway. The flat countryside all around made it easy to build since there was no need for extensive cutting and embanking and allowed a ruler straight path from point to point. Come July both verges of the line here are a glorious profusion of field scabious, St John's wort and Our Lady's bed straw. Soon there is more railway evidence. A concrete gate hanging and wire straining post for a farm occupation level crossing on the left. Following this a metal gate across the track opens onto a low embankment. Go through this gate and the subsequent hunt gate into a heavily wooded section. Here a brick, steel and concrete culvert in fine condition allows the Langford Brook through the embankment. Recognisable railway fencing now appears on both sides and as the undergrowth thins there is another farm level crossing with the original GWR gate hanging defiantly in use on the left side. The track, now level with the fields, soon reaches another farm and footpath occupation level crossing. Another broken hinged but original GWR gate hangs on the right where there is also a recycled rail wire straining post. In the thorn hedges on either side are the wooden GWR stiles, more or less in working order but obscured by the growth.

The line continues dead straight into the site of Langford station which was opened in 1907. The trackbed has been infilled with rubble and soil but the brick platform edge is easily discerned on the left. On the right the concrete uprights of the livestock loading pen still stand. Two tall cast concrete lamp posts denote the rear of the platform. The station approach is intact. At the far end a brick, steel and stone overbridge carries the lane between Langford and Grafton. The parapet is a cheap wood and corrugated iron affair. Cost cutting was a feature of the branch construction. To reduce the amount of material needed to build the approach ramps to overbridges the track bed was dug out so that the line dipped beneath each bridge. This is very obvious in contemporary photographs and often led to flooding of the line below bridges. Sure enough, even in high summer water usually lies beneath this bridge. The station building was made entirely of corrugated iron and has completely disappeared. Go through the metal gate under the bridge and continue along the line which again seems to be no more than a farm track level with the fields on the right although railway fence posts are just visible in the hedge on the left. Another GWR farm access gate appears on the left and in the hedge beside it another GWR wooden stile for the footpath which here crosses the line. The track now runs onto a low embankment and yet another GWR gate hangs on the left side with an associated redundant rail wire straining

Langford Brook Culvert, Fairford Branch

Langford Station Bridge, Fairford Branch

post. These gates have survived because they were built to last and very well maintained in their time. In addition they have been rarely used since the 1960's because the livestock which used to push and shove against them has all but disappeared from this now largely arable area. An all brick culvert takes a drainage ditch through the embankment followed by a large steel, brick and concrete culvert for the Broadwell Brook. Go through the metal gate beneath the next overbridge and turn sharp left off the line onto the stone farm road then turn right on the one track lane carried by the bridge. The latter is identical to that at Langford save that the parapets are angle iron and corrugated iron. The branch continues towards Alvescot.

Stay on the lane past Broadwell Mill on the left then at the 90 degree right hand bend follow the green metal footpath sign on the left over the wooden stile into the field. Turn left and follow the headland clockwise round the first field corner and beside the mixed alder, ash and willow trees which mark the course of the Broadwell Brook. Take the wooden plank foot bridge over the brook on the left and follow the headland of the subsequent permanent pasture clockwise towards the now visible buildings of Langford village. Cross the wooden stile beside the metal gate at the first field corner and follow the track with the high stone wall on the right hand. Cross Church Row and turn left along the pavement then turn right through the blue wrought iron gates into the yard of St Matthew's Church. Follow the paved stone path past the church door and cross the wooden stile in the church yard wall, walk down the steps and into the gravel lane opposite which leads to a metal kissing gate. Once through the kissing gate into the small ridge and furrow permanent pasture make for the wooden stile in the hedge at the far right hand corner. Cross the stile and follow the headland of the next field anti-clockwise then go through the metal gate at the first field corner. Turn left and follow the headland of this field clockwise to the second corner then turn left to cross the stone foot bridge over the ditch and turn right along the headland of the next field passing under the electricity pylon line then through the gate with the copse on the left. Turn left along the front of the copse, go through the double metal gates straight ahead and onto the grass farm track in the next field. This grass track is the public footpath which leads to and crosses the branch line just after the Langford Brook. Once on the line turn right and follow it back to Crossing Cottage and the parking place.

THE DURSLEY BRANCH LINE
(Dursley, Gloucestershire)

Map Sheet Ordnance Survey Explorer 167
Distance 3 and three quarter miles

Enter Dursley on the A4135 road from Tetbury. At the town centre with the Church of St James on the right the A4135 becomes a pedestrian only precinct and all traffic is taken round a semi circle to the right past the fire station before rejoining the A4135 boldly signed for Gloucester. Follow it until the second right marked by individual signs for various destinations including Lister Petter Ltd, Upper Cam & Coaley, Cam Congregational Church and St George's Church. The road is called Kingshill Lane. Follow it down a steep hill round a sharp left hand bend then park on the coarse gravel area on the right side of the road before the sharp right hand bend. The hump visible behind the wire netting fence at the edge of the gravel is all that remains of an embankment leading to a substantial bridge, now entirely removed, which carried the Dursley Branch Line over the road just after the right hand bend mentioned above.

Statue on the Market House, Dursley

The Dursley Branch Line opened 1856 and was operated by the Midland Railway Company (MR). It began at the MR main line at Coaley Junction and ran for 2 and a half miles to the centre of Dursley through one intermediate station at Lower Cam. Following the post Great War railway reorganisation the branch became part of the London, Midland & Scottish Railway Company (LM &SR).

During the Nineteenth Century the valley in which Dursley lies beneath the Cotswold escarpment had much in common with the Nailsworth and Stroud valleys to the north including a concentration of cloth mills, human and animal feed stuff processors, dye and chemical mixers along with plentiful labour nearby. There was also the influential and still surviving Lister family firm then making farm tools and implements for a national market. These economic conditions supported a prosperous branch line with a number of private mill sidings and work for 7 to 9 trains per day,goods rather than passengers being very much the main cargo. The line was closed in 1968 but Coaley Junction, now renamed Cam & Dursley, survives as a station on the main line.

From the parking place continue down hill and straight on along the right hand pavement of Everlands Road. The course of the branch is beside the pavement in a very shallow cutting now well grown with ash trees. Rising over the line is an occupation foot bridge in robust condition but closed to avert third party liability risks. The design is Victorian and unusual but some of the materials are comparatively modern. In common with other extant engineering works on the walk this bridge was largely rebuilt after the Second War. Take the footpath across the track below the bridge indicated by the green tin sign, go straight over the narrow grass paddock, cross the River Cam via the bridge and go through the wrought iron stile. Follow the now tarmac footpath between the new houses, turn left on the road then second right into the cul de sac, notice the next green tin sign on the pavement to the right and follow it into the grave yard of St George's Church. Take the path through the grave yard with the church on the right and the National Schools building on the left, go through the wrought iron gate onto Hopton Load and turn left along the pavement. Hopton Lane inclines gently down hill and behind the mixture of old and new houses on the left the River Cam runs along the valley bottom which marks the course of the branch line. Take the footpath over Hopton Green leaving the War Memorial on the right. Fork left downhill at the Y junction onto Station Road. At the foot of the short hill the road crosses the River Cam. On the Hopton Lane side of the bridge the branch crossed the road via a level crossing and the brick built Lower Cam Station was on the immediate right of the road. The open tarmac area to the left was the site of a private industrial siding. Nothing remains of all this but to record and celebrate it the Railway Inn stands on the other side of the Cam. The present landlord has some interesting family photographs showing the station just after closure of the branch and excellent framed photographs of the line from earlier periods are on the bar walls. Take the first right beyond the inn, called Rowley, which debouches onto the aptly named Chapel Street. Turn right along the pavement, join the A4135 and leaving the shopping complex on the right and the Berkeley Arms on the left follow the footpath sign on the right just past the A.S.Winterbotham Memorial Hall. Follow the tarmac path to the left of the reed lake, cross the River Cam on the concrete bridge and the track bed is to the front. Heavily overgrown but entirely intact is a farm and footpath underbridge. Note that the lower part of the abutments are original brick and stone but the upper works are modern concrete, which is why they are in such good condition. Cross the line and the wooden stile at the left of the gate and make for the far left hand corner of the permanent pasture. Cross the wooden stile there and turn left along the headland to the next stile in the thorn hedge. Cross it and turn left along the stone farm track noting an identical farm occupation underbridge beside the semi derelict factory with a mill race on the right. The factory is a good example of just why the branch line was pushed up the Dursley valley.

Recross the Cam on another concrete bridge, go straight through the new housing on the far side, rejoin the A4135, turn right along the pavement and follow it for half a mile. Draycott Mill Industrial Park appears on the right and beside the road is a Royal Mail depot. At the end of the depot security fence turn right at the footpath sign then left along the road under the electricity pylons then right again at the electricity transformer down the tarmac footpath between the industrial units. The footpath leads to a large multi arched underbridge carrying the line over the River Cam. Again the abutments and buttresses are MR brick and stone but the span and pillars are recent concrete in very good order. It is possible to view the now private track bed by scrambling up the embankment at the Coaley Junction end of the bridge. Cross the Cam on the footbridge and follow the well beaten path to the far right hand corner of the field. The line embankment leading away from the bridge forms the enclosure of this field on the right. Go through the gap in the hedge and continue on the well beaten path to the tree line opposite. Cross the wooden stile into and turn right on the stone farm track then leave it via the previously encountered stile in the hedge on the left. Follow the headland anticlockwise to the nearest, again already used, stile and cross it then turn sharp left keeping the hedge below the triple power cable at the left hand. To the right the ground falls away and the perimeter of the railway again forms part of the enclosure. Cross the next stile, follow the path straight ahead under the lime trees, go through the stile in the wire on the right, turn left on the tarmac drive then right down hill on the public road to the junction where Hopton Lane joins Station Road. Turn left along Hopton Lane to return to Kingshill Lane.

Everlands Foot Bridge, Dursley Branch

River Cam Bridge, Dursley Branch

BIBLIOGRAPHY

Abbott D. & Robertson K. - The Marlborough Branch, Irwell Press
Bray N. - The Cirencester Branch, The Oakwood Press
Fenton M. - The Malmesbury Branch, White Swan Publications Ltd
Judge C.W. - Great Western Branch Lines, The Oakwood Press
Maggs C.G. - The Nailsworth & Stroud Branch, The Oakwood Press
Maggs C.G. - The Calne Branch, White Swan Publications Ltd
Mitchell V. & Smith K. - Branch Line To Fairford, Middleton Press
Randolph S. - The Tetbury Branch, White Swan Publications Ltd
Sands T.B. - The Midland & South Western Junction Railway,
The Oakwood Press